JAMES
MADISON

AMERICA'S FOURTH PRESIDENT

BY TAMARA ORR STAATS

Boston, Massachusetts
Chandler, Arizona
Glenview, Illinois
Upper Saddle River, New Jersey

Illustrations
2 (T), 9, 10, 11, 12 Len Ebert.

Photographs
Every effort has been made to secure permission and provide appropriate credit for photographic material.
The publisher deeply regrets any omission and pledges to correct errors called to its attention in subsequent editions.

Unless otherwise acknowledged, all photographs are the property of Pearson Education, Inc.

Photo locators denoted as follows: Top (T), Center (C), Bottom (B), Left (L), Right (R), Background (Bkgd)

Opener: Prints & Photographs Division, LC-DIG-ppmsca-19166/Library of Congress; 1 Prints & Photographs Division, LC-DIG-ppmsca-19166/Library of Congress; 2 Thinkstock; 4 Prints & Photographs Division, LC-USZC4-1583/Library of Congress; 5 Prints & Photographs Division, LC-DIG-pga-03359/Library of Congress; 6 Prints & Photographs Division, LC-DIG-ppmsca-05483/Library of Congress; 7 Theodor Horydczak Collection, Prints & Photographs Division, LC-H8-CT-V05-002/Library of Congress; 8 Prints & Photographs Division, LC-USZC4-9904/Library of Congress; 13 Photolibrary Group, Inc.; 14 Prints & Photographs Division, LC-USZ62-68175/Library of Congress; 15 Prints & Photographs Division, LC-DIG-ppmsca-30581/Library of Congress.

ISBN-13: 978-0-328-67632-3
ISBN-10: 0-328-67632-2

10 11 12   18 17 16

Little Jemmy

James Madison was a small, shy boy. He had a soft voice, and he was often sick. His father called him "Little Jemmy." As a grown man, he did not have a large or strong body.

James Madison was our fourth president.

However, Madison did grow up to be a strong leader with a strong mind. He was the fourth president of the United States. Before that, he helped plan the government we have today.

Growing Up

James Madison was born on March 16, 1751, in the British **colony** of Virginia. He lived on a large farm with a view of the Blue Ridge Mountains. His family was wealthy.

Because Madison was often sick, he spent a lot of time indoors. He loved to read. By the time he was 11 years old, he had read all 85 books in his father's library.

The Madison family lived within view of the Blue Ridge Mountains.

Education

Madison's father sent him away to school. Young Madison was happy there. He studied French, Latin, Greek, history, and mathematics.

When Madison was sixteen, he came home. All the talk was about the new **taxes** Great Britain was making the colonies pay. People were upset.

Colonists were upset about the new taxes.

The College of New Jersey

In 1769 Madison left home again and rode off on his horse to the College of New Jersey. This college is now called Princeton University. Despite his shyness, Madison made many friends there. He was an excellent student, too.

Revolution

Madison finished college in two years and came home. People were still upset about taxes. Many people wanted the colonies to gain **independence**. In April 1775, fighting broke out in Lexington, Massachusetts. Colonists fought British soldiers. The American **Revolution** had begun.

The Battle of Lexington

Madison and other leaders worked in the capitol in Williamsburg, Virginia.

Working for Virginia

Back in Virginia, people were thinking about planning a new government. Madison was chosen to help write a new **constitution**. Madison had strong opinions. He believed strongly in the right of people to worship freely. He made sure that the freedom of religion was protected in Virginia's constitution.

Late in 1777, Madison was chosen to be part of a group of people advising the governor of Virginia. Madison worked closely with Thomas Jefferson. Just the year before, Jefferson had written the Declaration of Independence. This was a statement to the British saying that the colonies were free. Madison and Jefferson became lifelong friends.

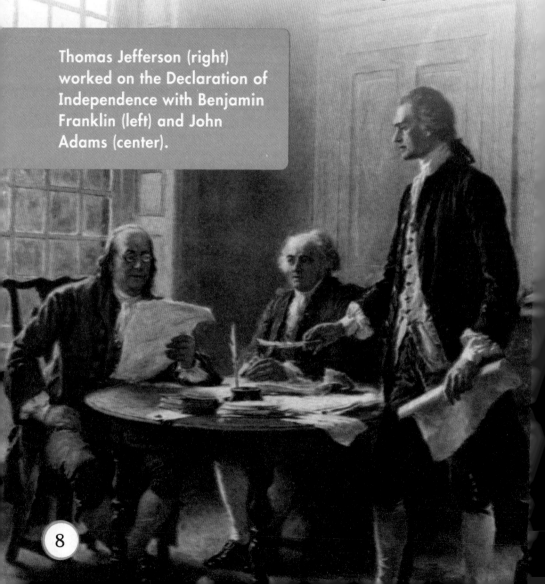

Thomas Jefferson (right) worked on the Declaration of Independence with Benjamin Franklin (left) and John Adams (center).

A Weak Plan

In 1780, Madison went to Philadelphia to help plan a government for the new country. Many of the leaders were afraid of a strong central government. After all, they were fighting to be free of the British king. So the government they designed gave most of the power to the states. The plan was called the Articles of Confederation. Madison was not happy with it. He didn't think it would work very well.

Under the Articles of Confederation, each state printed its own money.

The British surrender

Finally, in 1783, the war was over. Americans had won their independence!

But Madison was worried. He had studied history and government for many years. He was sure that the Articles of Confederation were too weak. It wasn't long before Madison was proved right. People could see that the plan wasn't working.

A New Plan

In 1787, fifty-five of the country's leaders met in Philadelphia. They were supposed to fix the Articles and make them stronger.

Madison was there too. Every day he took notes. Thanks to him we have a very good idea of what happened.

George Washington was in charge of the meeting.

Madison didn't think it was possible to fix the Articles. Instead, he had a new plan all ready. His plan had a strong central government with three branches that shared power.

All summer long the leaders argued about the plan. They made many **compromises**. Finally, in September, they agreed on a plan. Many of Madison's ideas remained in it. The United States now had a new Constitution.

Three Branches of Government

Executive

Legislative

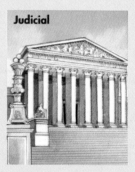
Judicial

Under the United States Constitution, the three branches of government share power.

The Bill of Rights

The Constitution needed nine states to approve it. But several states said no. They objected because the Constitution did not have a list of rights.

So Madison wrote a set of **amendments**, or changes, to the Constitution. These first ten amendments became known as the Bill of Rights. By 1790, all 13 states had approved the Constitution.

The Bill of Rights protects freedom of the press. This means newspapers can write about any topic.

Dolley Madison

On September 15, 1794, Madison surprised many people. He got married! Dolley Madison was very friendly and charming. When James Madison became the president in 1809, Dolley Madison loved entertaining people at the White House.

Dolley Madison

President Madison

During Madison's time as president, the United States fought another war against Great Britain. In 1814 British troops entered Washington, D.C. They set fire to much of the city. Madison barely escaped. The war ended with a peace agreement in December 1814.

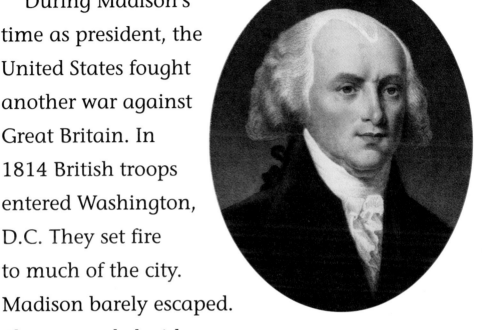

Today Madison is remembered best for his work in designing our government. He is known as the "Father of the Constitution."

Glossary

amendment a change or an addition to the
   Constitution

colony a place ruled by another country

compromise the settling of a disagreement by
   each side giving up some of what it wants

constitution a written plan for government

independence freedom from another country's
   rule

revolution a war fought to replace one
   government with another one

tax money paid to a government